Christmas Hy[gge]
Coloring Book
Bold and Easy

By Jeannie Mac Media

Color Test

Deck the Halls!

Hygge

Pronounced Hue-guh

Hygge

A Danish and Norwegian word.

Hygge means comfort.

Santa Claus is reading his naughty and nice list.

5

Santa is making cookies!

Cozy Comfort

Drinking Hot Chocolate

8

Posing for a picture

9

Reading about Rudolph

Sugar Cookies....YUM!

Getting into the Christmas Spirit

For Me?

Coffee for a snowman???

The Sloth Getting in on
The Christmas Joy!

Candy canes for All!

Rudolph?

Comfort for my tootsies

Marshmallows!

19

A Beary Joyful Christmas

A Beary, Beary Joyful
Christmas indeed!

A Rabbit Wreath

Trimming the Tree

Baking Cookies
A Christmas Tradition

Hot Chocolate with Marshmallows!

Jolly Old Saint Nicholas

"'Twas the Night Before Christmas"

Santa is making something special.

Just a Swinging!

Roasting Marshmallows

A Visit From the Wise Owl

A Hedgehog with his Lantern

Let it Snow!

Snowball Fun!

Tweet Tweet. Thanks for Coloring!

Made in the USA
Columbia, SC
05 December 2024

48486415R00041